MW00648644

Sacagawea
A Sign of Peace

by Mary Ann Ryan
illustrated by Leslie Bowman

Harcourt

SCHOOL PUBLISHERS

Requests for permission to make copies of any part of the work should be addressed to School Permissions and Copyrights, Harcourt, Inc., 6277 Sea Harbor Drive, Orlando, Florida 32887–6777. Fax: 407-345-2418.

HARCOURT and the Harcourt Logo are trademarks of Harcourt, Inc., registered in the United States of America and/or other jurisdictions.

Printed in China

ISBN 10: 0-15-351678-X
ISBN 13: 978-0-15-351678-8

Ordering Options
ISBN 10: 0-15-351215-6 (Grade 5 Advanced Collection)
ISBN 13: 978-0-15-351215-5 (Grade 5 Advanced Collection)
ISBN 10: 0-15-358161-1 (package of 5)
ISBN 13: 978-0-15-358161-8 (package of 5)

4 5 6 7 8 9 10   0940   12 11 10 09

Westward Expansion

In the year 1803, the United States bought thousands of square miles of land from France in the Louisiana Purchase. This sparked much interest in westward expansion. President Thomas Jefferson convinced Congress to give him the necessary money to fund a journey to explore "to the western ocean." Explorers were to study Native Americans, plants and animals, and the land in the region.

The team of Lewis and Clark and their "Corps of Discovery" were chosen for this journey. The expedition lasted four years and covered more than four thousand miles (6,437 km). However, without the help of a young Native American woman named Sacagawea, Lewis and Clark may not have survived to tell about it.

Sacagawea's Early Life

Sacagawea was born around 1789 near present-day Montana. She lived with her Shoshone tribe on the western side of the Rocky Mountains where Idaho is today. When Sacagawea was a young girl, she was kidnapped by a group of warriors from the Hidatsa tribe. The Hidatsa often would attack the Shoshone, steal their horses, and take prisoners.

Both Lewis and Clark kept separate journals of the expedition. In fact, most of what we know about Sacagawea comes from these writings. One recorded event had to do with Sacagawea's quick thinking. Since the group traveled by foot and by canoe, it was not uncommon for them to encounter problems. At one point, the harsh weather put the expedition in peril. The canoe in which Sacagawea, Charbonneau, and their baby were riding almost tipped over. As the men panicked and bailed water from the boat, Sacagawea remained calm and went into the water to save clothing, books, a microscope, and the captains' important journals. After the ordeal, Lewis described Sacagawea in his journal as both loyal and brave.

As time went on, the trip to the mountains became much more difficult to endure. The expedition had to cross the Great Falls of the Missouri River. Although this leg of the journey covered only eighteen miles (29 km), because of the harsh terrain and even harsher conditions, it took an entire month.

There seemed to be one disaster after another. The group had to carry their canoes and supplies around several waterfalls. The terrain was treacherous and the weather dismal. It rained profusely, sometimes for days at a time. The group was often caught unsheltered in fierce storms. Hailstones pelted so hard that some members of the party were seriously injured. The weather grew colder each day. By the summer of 1805, Lewis and Clark still had not reached the mountains, and time was getting short.

After passing the Great Falls of the Missouri River, the group found themselves on the eastern side of the Rocky Mountains. There the explorers came upon a place that looked as if the river had carved a road through solid rock. As the expedition paddled through the area, Lewis and Clark looked for signs that they were near the Shoshones. They hoped that Sacagawea would recognize the area.

Lewis and Clark divided their team and set out to find the river fork that would lead them through the mountains to the Columbia River. While the men were out scouting the countryside, Sacagawea made a startling discovery. She realized that she recognized this place. Their campsite was the very place where she had been kidnapped by the Hidatsa years earlier.

Lewis set off on foot with some of the men to find the Shoshone. The rest of the party traveled either by foot or by canoe with the bulk of the supplies.

Then one day, as Sacagawea was walking along the shoreline, a group of Shoshones rode toward her on horseback. She watched them intently and knew that she recognized them. Sacagawea had found her people!

While Sacagawea visited with her lost friends, the explorers held a council with the Shoshone chief, Cameahwait. When Sacagawea was called in to interpret, she was unable to speak. Instead, she fell into the arms of the chief and began to cry. Chief Cameahwait was, in fact, her long lost brother! The men stood speechless in the presence of this joyous reunion.

Along the expedition, whenever Lewis and Clark met with Indians, they gave them presents that included American flags and Jefferson medals known as "peace medals."

Lewis and Clark explained their plans to the Shoshone council. They told the chief that the United States Government wanted to begin trading with Native Americans. They explained why they needed to find a route through the mountains. They presented the Shoshone with gifts from President Jefferson.

In return, Chief Cameahwait decided to trade for horses. He gave Lewis and Clark a detailed description of the route to follow to the Columbia River. The Shoshone explained that a water route was impossible and that they would have to cross the mountains on horseback. With the help of Sacagawea, Lewis and Clark acquired twenty-nine horses from the Shoshone. On September 4, 1805, Sacagawea said a tearful good-bye to her brother and her people.

The expedition continued on northwest across what is now Montana and Idaho, and Sacagawea continued on, too. In each part of the journey, every group of Native Americans they encountered offered help. In all accounts, this was because of Sacagawea. According to Clark, to Native Americans, a woman's presence with a group of men was a "sign of peace."

Each time the expedition met a new group of Native Americans, the sight of Sacagawea and her son, Jean Baptiste, confirmed that their group was friendly and not a war party. In fact, if it hadn't been for the goodwill of the Native Americans, many in the party may not have survived. Native Americans along the way shared their food and shelter. Most importantly, they pointed the expedition in the right direction.

By this time, the journey was one raging river and death-defying waterfall after another. The explorers navigated their way down the Clearwater and Snake Rivers until they finally reached the Columbia River. The Columbia River led them to their goal—the Pacific Ocean. There they spent the winter.

September 10, 1805, Meriwether Lewis

The Indians were mounted on very fine horses of which [they] have a great abundance; that is, each man in the nation possesses from 20 to a hundred head.

The sun was now set, two of them departed . . . and the third remained, having agreed to continue with us as a guide, and to introduce us to his relations whom he informed us were numerous and resided in the plain below the mountains on the Columbia River, from whence he said the water was good and capable of being navigated to the sea.

The Pacific Coast

During the long cold winter along the Pacific coastline, Sacagawea was again resourceful. Over the length of the journey, most of their clothing had become worn and rotted. Using animal skins and her sewing skills, Sacagawea made new shirts and moccasins for the members of the expedition.

As spring approached, Lewis and Clark and their party were ready to return home and report on their findings. They had left St. Louis, Missouri, in May of 1804. In March of 1806, they began the long trip back. Once the snow had melted, Lewis and Clark followed new trails back in order to explore the Yellowstone River. On the way, they saw many of the same people who had helped them along their journey.

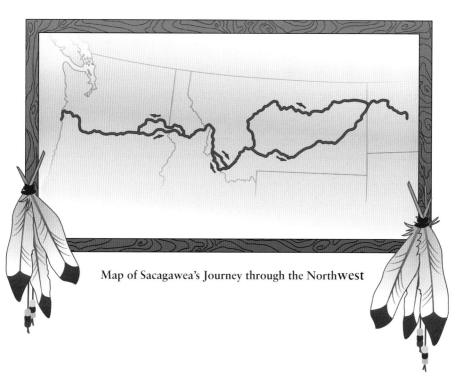

Map of Sacagawea's Journey through the Northwest

On their return, Lewis and Clark prepared their report for President Jefferson. A small delegation from the expedition accompanied them to Washington, D.C. The rest of the group disbanded. Charbonneau was paid five hundred dollars for his services to Lewis and Clark. Sacagawea, on the other hand, was paid nothing at all.

Remembering Sacagawea

Sacagawea made a great contribution to Lewis and Clark's expedition. In their journals, they recorded what they saw. They described close to two hundred types of fruits, flowers, and trees. Many of these Sacagawea had told them about. They also included drawings of more than one hundred animals that, at the time, were undocumented. These included coyotes, porcupines, and prairie dogs, which were all unfamiliar to Lewis and Clark, but were recognizable to Sacagawea.

No one really knows what happened to Sacagawea, although legends and stories give different accounts about the remainder of her life. Some say she returned to the Shoshone and became a revered elder, living to be almost one hundred years old. Others say she died shortly after her return from the expedition in South Dakota.

More important than the age at which she died was the spirit in which Sacagawea lived. Without her calm, kind, and resourceful ways, we may have never known the success of Lewis and Clark's expedition.

Think Critically

1. What were two ways that Sacagawea proved beneficial to the expedition?

2. Summarize this book in several sentences.

3. How was the expedition difficult and brutal?

4. Why was Sacagawea considered "a sign of peace"?

5. What do you think would have happened to the expedition had Lewis and Clark not encountered Sacagawea along the way?

 Social Studies

Make a Lewis and Clark Puzzle Design a crossword puzzle. Use words and information from the story. Write a clue for each word. Your puzzle should include at least eight words—four across and four down. Exchange puzzles with a friend.

School-Home Connection With your family, discuss Sacagawea and her journey. Make a list of the character traits she must have had in order to make the trip and get along with the people on the expedition.

Word Count: 1,821